THE GPT-RENEUR

USING ARTIFICIAL INTELLIGENCE TO UNLOCK PROFITABLE NICHES

By Alexander J. Kelley

The GPT-Reneur: Using Artificial Intelligence to Unlock Profitable Niches

Copyright © 2023 by Alexander J. Kelley

Book Cover by Alexander J. Kelley

First Edition 2023

www.alexanderkelley.com

To my Dad, Jim.
My first memory of computers came from watching you tinker
at home with one, and learning how to play games from cutting
edge floppy drives. I enjoyed sharing your passion with you.
I love you, Dad.

Table of Contents

Introduction

Introduction

Welcome to The GPT-Reneur

Welcome to ***The GPT-Reneur***, a comprehensive guide to harnessing the power of artificial intelligence (AI) for business planning and ideation. In today's rapidly evolving business landscape, coming up with unique and innovative business ideas can be a challenging task. This difficulty can lead to missed opportunities and even failure for businesses that do not keep up with the competition.

However, AI has the potential to assist in the ideation and planning process by generating new ideas and analyzing market data. This book is designed to help entrepreneurs and business professionals understand how AI can be used for business planning and ideation.

In this book, we will explore the potential of AI-generated business ideas and how they can be assessed for viability. We will also discuss how AI can assist in creating a well-written business plan and explore the challenges and limitations of using AI in business planning. Additionally, we will examine case studies of real-world examples of AI-driven business planning and ideation and explore ethical considerations for the use of AI in business.

Furthermore, we will explore the role of human input and expertise in AI-driven business planning and ideation and examine strategies for balancing AI with human contributions. Finally, we will discuss how AI can be used beyond the planning phase to support business implementation and execution.

By the end of this book, you will have a comprehensive understanding of how AI can be used for business planning and ideation. You will also have a deep understanding of the benefits and limitations of using AI in business, as well as the strategies and best practices for effectively integrating AI into your business planning processes. Let's get started!

Coming Up with Unique Business Ideas Is Hard

Starting a business can be an exciting and challenging endeavor, and one of the biggest hurdles that aspiring entrepreneurs face is coming up with unique and innovative business ideas. With so many businesses already in existence, it can be difficult to identify untapped markets or come up with a product or service that sets a new standard.

One of the main reasons for the difficulty in generating unique business ideas is the lack of knowledge and expertise in a particular industry or field. Entrepreneurs may have a general idea of what they want to do, but they may not have the expertise or understanding of a particular market to develop an innovative and successful business idea. Another challenge is the overwhelming amount of information available, which can make it difficult to identify gaps in the market and find inspiration.

Fortunately, advancements in artificial intelligence (AI) have made it possible for entrepreneurs to generate unique business ideas and overcome these challenges. AI can assist in the ideation and planning process by providing valuable insights, market research, and identification of gaps in existing markets. With the help of AI, entrepreneurs can generate new and innovative ideas in untapped niches and create successful businesses.

One of the ways AI can help entrepreneurs generate business ideas is using machine learning algorithms that can analyze large amounts of data and identify patterns and trends. This can be useful in identifying market gaps and consumer needs that can be fulfilled through new products or services. AI-powered market research tools can also provide insights into consumer behavior, trends, and preferences, which can be valuable in developing unique and innovative business ideas.

Case studies of successful businesses that have used AI for idea generation demonstrate the effectiveness of this approach. For example, the clothing brand Stitch Fix uses AI algorithms to analyze customer data and identify clothing items that are likely to appeal to individual customers. The company has been highly successful, with a reported annual revenue of over $1 billion.

However, it's important to note that AI-generated business ideas must still be assessed for their viability and potential success. This involves evaluating market demand, forecasting potential sales, and assessing risks. AI can assist in this process by providing market analysis, forecasting, and risk assessment tools. By leveraging AI-powered insights, entrepreneurs can create a well-informed and realistic business plan that increases their chances of success.

Despite the benefits of AI in generating and assessing business ideas, there are also limitations and potential issues to consider. AI-generated ideas may not always be practical or feasible, and there is still a need for human input and expertise in evaluating ideas and developing business plans. Additionally, there are ethical considerations related to the use of AI in business planning and ideation.

While the difficulty of coming up with unique business ideas can be a significant hurdle for entrepreneurs, advancements in AI have made it possible to overcome this challenge. By leveraging AI-powered tools for idea generation, market research, and risk assessment, entrepreneurs can create successful businesses in untapped niches. However, it's important to balance the use of AI with human input and expertise and to ensure that ethical considerations are accounted for throughout the process.

Introduction

Let AI Imagine & Plan Your Next Business Venture

Artificial intelligence (AI) is revolutionizing the way businesses operate, and it is now being increasingly used in the ideation and planning process. Traditional methods of ideation and planning often relied on intuition and human expertise, which can be limited by personal biases and the availability of data. In contrast, AI can analyze vast amounts of data quickly and accurately, which can provide insights and identify opportunities that may have been missed otherwise.

One way in which AI can assist in ideation is by generating new business ideas in untapped niches. With access to vast amounts of data, AI-powered algorithms can identify gaps in existing markets and suggest new business opportunities. For instance, AI-powered market research tools can analyze consumer trends and identify new product or service categories that have high potential for growth.

AI can also assist in the planning process by analyzing data and forecasting market trends. This can help businesses make informed decisions about where to invest resources and what strategies to pursue. By analyzing historical data and real-time market data, AI-powered algorithms can predict future trends and identify potential risks, which can help businesses make better decisions.

One example of how AI is being used in the planning process is in financial forecasting. AI-powered algorithms can analyze financial data, such as revenue & expenses, and use this information to generate financial projections. These projections can help businesses make informed decisions about where to allocate resources and identify areas for improvement.

Another way in which AI can assist in the planning process is by automating certain tasks, such as data entry and analysis. This can free up time for employees to focus on more strategic tasks, such as identifying new business opportunities and developing marketing strategies.

AI can also help businesses optimize their operations by identifying areas for improvement. For instance, AI-powered algorithms can analyze supply chain data and identify inefficiencies or bottlenecks that are causing delays or increasing costs. This information can then be used to optimize processes and improve efficiency.

However, while AI can provide significant benefits in the ideation and planning process, it is not a panacea. AI-generated ideas may be limited by the data that is available and may not consider the unique perspectives and experiences of human entrepreneurs. It is important to recognize the limitations of AI and ensure that human expertise is still valued and integrated into the ideation and planning process.

In addition, there are also concerns about the ethical implications of using AI in the ideation and planning process. For instance, some may worry that the use of AI could perpetuate existing biases or lead to unintended consequences. It is important to ensure that the use of AI is ethical and that it does not harm individuals or communities.

Despite these concerns, the potential benefits of AI in the ideation and planning process cannot be ignored. AI can provide valuable insights and identify opportunities that may have been missed otherwise. By combining human expertise with AI-generated insights, businesses can create more effective and innovative strategies for success.

In conclusion, AI has the potential to significantly impact the ideation and planning process. By analyzing data and providing insights, AI-powered algorithms can help businesses identify new opportunities and make informed decisions. However, it is important to recognize the limitations of AI and ensure that human expertise is integrated into the process. Ultimately, the combination of AI and human expertise can lead to more effective and innovative business strategies.

Chapter 1 - AI - Generated Business Ideas

Chapter 1

How Can AI Help Me Find Ideas in Untapped Niches?

Artificial intelligence has made significant advancements in recent years, and one of its most valuable applications is in generating new business ideas. Traditional methods of market research and ideation often result in ideas that are not unique or innovative, leaving many entrepreneurs struggling to find new opportunities in untapped markets or niches. However, AI provides a new way of approaching the ideation process, using algorithms to identify gaps in existing markets and generate novel ideas.

AI-powered market research involves analyzing large amounts of data to identify patterns and trends that are not easily discernible by humans. With the vast amount of data available on the internet, AI algorithms can quickly sift through vast amounts of information to identify gaps in the market that can be exploited. By analyzing data from social media, e-commerce platforms, and search engines, AI algorithms can identify emerging trends and areas of consumer demand that traditional market research methods may miss.

AI can also be used to generate new business ideas by identifying patterns in existing successful businesses. Machine learning algorithms can analyze large datasets of successful businesses and identify patterns that can be used to create new ideas. These algorithms can analyze data from various industries, such as finance, retail, or healthcare, and use that information to generate new business ideas that have the potential to disrupt the market.

Another way AI generates new business ideas is through natural language processing (NLP). NLP is a branch of AI that focuses on understanding and interpreting human language. By analyzing customer reviews, comments on social media, and other forms of customer feedback, AI algorithms can identify common pain points or unmet needs that can be addressed with new products or services. This approach can lead to innovative solutions to longstanding problems, creating entirely new markets or niches.

AI can also be used to create new business models by identifying patterns in existing business models and using that information to create something new. Machine learning algorithms can analyze existing businesses, identify gaps in their business model, and use that information to create a new business model. For example, AI algorithms can identify businesses that operate on a subscription model and use that information to create a new subscription-based business model that targets a different market or niche.

While search engines like Google and Bing are great for finding specific information, AI chatbots like ChatGPT, Chatsonic, and Google Bard AI can provide personalized responses and generate ideas based on the context and details of your specific situation.

Artificial Intelligence chatbots use natural language processing to understand the nuances and complexities of human language. This means that you can interact with them using natural language in a way that feels more like a conversation than a search engine. You can ask follow up questions, the can give you probing responses.

Here are three sample prompts you can use to harness the power of artificial intelligence to help you come up with some niche ideas for your next business. Done properly, your chatbot should begin asking you some follow up questions to help you get closer to finding your idea. Don't be afraid to mix & match questions, and test the output results:

1. "Can you assist me in identifying untapped niches that have potential for a new business venture?"
2. "I am looking to create a new business, but I am struggling to find untapped niches. Can you help me with that?"
3. "How can you help me discover untapped niches that I can explore to start a new business?"
4. "I am seeking your guidance to find untapped niches that I can explore and build a new business. Can you assist me?"
5. "What approach can I take to leverage your knowledge and expertise in finding untapped niches that can be a potential opportunity for a new business?"

In conclusion, AI has tremendous potential in generating new business ideas in untapped niches. With its ability to analyze vast amounts of data, identify emerging trends, and understand human language, AI algorithms can help entrepreneurs identify gaps in existing markets and create new business ideas. By leveraging the power of AI, entrepreneurs can stay ahead of the competition and create innovative solutions to longstanding problems, opening entirely new markets and niches.

Chapter 1

AI-Powered Market Research & Identification of Gaps in Existing Markets

In today's world, businesses are facing an increasing amount of competition, which makes it challenging for them to find untapped markets. Companies require a unique approach to identify new opportunities and stay ahead of their competition. AI-powered market research is the answer. AI technology enables businesses to use data-driven insights to make informed decisions and identify gaps in existing markets.

AI algorithms can collect, process, and analyze vast amounts of data, providing insights that businesses may have overlooked. These algorithms can identify market trends, consumer behavior, and competitive landscapes to help businesses find new opportunities. By using AI-powered market research, businesses can save time, resources, and money, as the research process is faster and more accurate.

One way that AI-powered market research can identify gaps in existing markets is by analyzing social media data. Social media platforms generate an immense amount of data that businesses can leverage. AI algorithms can analyze this data to identify consumer preferences, opinions, and behavior patterns. This analysis can help businesses identify gaps in the market, such as a particular product or service that consumers desire but is currently unavailable.

Another way that AI-powered market research can identify gaps in existing markets is through web scraping. Web scraping is a technique that involves using AI algorithms to extract data from websites. This data can be analyzed to identify trends, gaps in the market, and consumer behavior patterns. Web scraping can provide valuable insights into what consumers are searching for, their preferences, and what products or services are in high demand.

AI-powered market research can also help businesses identify gaps in the market by analyzing competitor data. AI algorithms can collect data on competitors, such as their product offerings, marketing strategies, and pricing. By analyzing this data, businesses can identify areas where they can differentiate themselves from their competitors and find new opportunities.

AI-powered market research has revolutionized the way businesses identify gaps in existing markets. It provides businesses with a more accurate, data-driven approach to market research, which can save time, resources, and money. The technology provides businesses with the insights they need to make informed decisions and identify new opportunities. By leveraging AI-powered market research, businesses can gain a competitive advantage in today's highly competitive business landscape.

Here are three sample prompts you can ask AI to help you gather market research:

1. "Can you assist me in conducting market research to identify potential gaps and opportunities for my business? How do I begin?"
2. "As a startup, I am looking for ways to conduct market research to gain insights into my target audience and competition. Can you guide me on how to use a chatbot for this purpose?"

3. "I'm not sure where to start with market research, but I want to find out more about my customers and competitors. Can you show me how to use a chatbot to gather this information?"

AI-powered market research can be a game-changer for businesses looking to identify untapped niches in existing markets. By analyzing social media data, web scraping, and competitor data, businesses can gain valuable insights into consumer behavior, preferences, and trends. These insights can help businesses identify gaps in the market and find new opportunities to differentiate themselves from their competitors. With AI-powered market research, businesses can make informed decisions that can lead to their success.

Chapter 1

Case Studies: Business Using AI for Idea Generation

Artificial Intelligence has emerged as a powerful tool for businesses of all sizes, providing valuable insights and assistance in a wide range of areas. One of the most important areas in which AI has proven to be particularly helpful is in the generation of new business ideas, particularly in untapped or overlooked niches. In this section, we will explore six case studies of successful businesses that have leveraged AI to generate new business ideas and achieve success.

1. Hugging Face: Hugging Face is a popular AI startup that has made a name for itself in the natural language processing (NLP) space. The company's flagship product is an open-source platform that enables developers to create and deploy AI-powered chatbots and virtual assistants. Hugging Face uses AI algorithms to analyze millions of conversations and provide developers with insights into user behavior, preferences, and pain points. By leveraging AI-powered market research and analysis, Hugging Face has been able to identify untapped niches in the NLP space and create innovative products that have been embraced by developers and consumers alike.

2. The Sill: The Sill is an online plant store that uses AI to analyze data on consumer behavior and market trends to generate new product ideas. By using AI-powered algorithms, The Sill can quickly identify emerging plant species and trending colors, shapes, and sizes, allowing them to introduce new products and stay ahead of the competition.

3. Hubble Contacts: Hubble Contacts is a direct-to-consumer contact lens company that used AI to identify gaps in the contact lens market. By analyzing consumer feedback and market trends, Hubble identified a need for affordable, high-quality contact lenses, which they now offer to customers through a subscription-based model.

4. Drizly: Drizly is an online alcohol delivery service that used AI to identify untapped markets for its products. By analyzing customer data and market trends, Drizly was able to identify new markets for its services and expand into new geographic areas, increasing its customer base and revenue.

5. Nectar Sleep: Nectar Sleep is an online mattress company that used AI to develop its product line. By analyzing data on customer preferences and sleeping patterns, Nectar Sleep was able to create a mattress that catered to a wider range of customers, resulting in increased sales and customer satisfaction.

6. Brandless: Brandless is an online retailer that offers a variety of household and grocery products at an affordable price point. Using AI, Brandless was able to identify popular product categories and trends, allowing them to quickly develop new products and expand their offerings to appeal to a wider range of consumers.

7. Pillo Health - Pillo Health is a healthcare company that uses AI-powered chatbots to help patients manage their medication schedules and provide personalized health recommendations. The company's AI technology analyzes patient data to identify potential health issues and provide personalized recommendations to improve their overall health. Pillo Health has been successful in leveraging AI

to create a unique niche in the healthcare industry, and their innovative approach has led to several awards and recognitions in the industry.

8. ThirdLove: A lingerie brand that uses AI algorithms to gather data from customers and recommend personalized bra sizes and styles. The company uses a Fit Finder quiz to collect data on customers' breast shape and size preferences. It also uses machine learning to analyze customer feedback and identify areas for product improvement. ThirdLove's use of AI has allowed them to offer a wider range of sizes and styles, leading to increased customer satisfaction and brand loyalty.

9. Lemonade: An insurance startup that uses AI to streamline the claims process and improve customer service. The company's AI-powered chatbot, Maya, can help customers file claims and answer questions 24/7. Lemonade uses machine learning algorithms to process claims faster and more accurately than traditional insurance companies. This has allowed the company to offer lower premiums and faster payouts, making them a popular choice for customers looking for affordable and efficient insurance solutions.

10. Hugging Face: A chatbot company that uses AI to power its language model and provide natural language processing capabilities. The company's chatbot can assist with a variety of tasks, from scheduling appointments to ordering food. Hugging Face's AI technology allows its chatbot to understand and respond to natural language queries, making it a more user-friendly and efficient alternative to traditional chatbots.

11. Stasher: A reusable silicone bag brand that uses AI to identify new market opportunities and optimize its advertising campaigns. The company uses machine learning algorithms to analyze customer behavior and identify patterns that can help improve its marketing efforts. Stasher's use of AI has allowed them to target specific customer segments with personalized marketing messages, leading to increased sales and customer loyalty.

12. Freenome: A healthcare startup that uses AI to detect early signs of cancer through blood tests. The company's AI algorithms analyze the genetic information in a patient's blood to identify potential cancer indicators. Freenome's use of AI has allowed them to offer a more accurate and cost-effective cancer screening solution, potentially saving lives through earlier detection and treatment.

Success stories like those listed above demonstrate the powerful impact of AI on idea generation, market research, customer service, and advertising. By utilizing the vast amounts of data available in the digital age and leveraging AI algorithms, these companies were able to identify untapped niches, improve their products and services, and connect with customers on a deeper level. Their innovative use of AI has allowed them to differentiate themselves in competitive markets and establish themselves as industry leaders.

As AI continues to advance and become more accessible, it is likely that we will see more and more businesses turn to AI-powered solutions for idea generation and market research.

Chapter 2 - Assessing the Viability of AI-Generated Business Ideas

Chapter 2

Evaluating Ideas Before Investing Time & Resources

Aspiring entrepreneurs are often full of ideas that they believe have great potential for success. However, not all business ideas are created equal, and investing time and resources into a venture without first evaluating its potential success can be a costly mistake. In this section, we'll explore the importance of evaluating the potential success of business ideas before investing time and resources and discuss some key factors to consider when doing so.

One key factor in evaluating the potential success of a business idea is the size of the target market. A business idea may seem brilliant, but if there is no viable market for the product or service, it will ultimately fail. Therefore, it's important to conduct market research to determine the size and potential growth of the target market, as well as the competition in the space.

Another factor to consider is the potential profitability of the business idea. This includes not only the potential revenue streams, but also the costs associated with operating the business. A business that generates a lot of revenue but also incurs significant expenses may not be as profitable as it initially seems. It's important to evaluate the potential revenue and expenses of the business and determine whether the potential profit margins are high enough to make the venture worthwhile.

The next factor to consider is the scalability of the business idea. A business that is not scalable may not be worth pursuing, as it may have limited potential for growth and expansion. Evaluating the scalability of the business idea requires considering the potential for growth, as well as the resources and infrastructure needed to support that growth.

Another important factor to consider is the feasibility of the business idea. This includes assessing whether the necessary resources and expertise are available to execute the idea, as well as whether the regulatory environment is favorable to the venture. It's also important to consider the potential risks and challenges associated with the business idea and determine whether they can be overcome.

In addition to these key factors, it's important to evaluate the market timing of the business idea. A business idea that is ahead of its time may not be successful, as there may not yet be sufficient demand for the product or service. Conversely, a business idea that is too late to the market may face stiff competition and struggle to gain traction. Therefore, it's important to assess the timing of the business idea and determine whether the market is ready for it.

Here are some additional free resources that can help aspiring entrepreneurs evaluate their business ideas before investing time and resources:

1. SCORE: SCORE is a nonprofit organization that offers free business advice and mentoring to entrepreneurs. They have a network of experienced volunteers who can help you evaluate the potential success of your business idea, develop a business plan, and more.

2. Small Business Development Centers (SBDCs): SBDCs are a nationwide network of centers that provide free counseling and resources to small business owners and aspiring entrepreneurs. They offer one-on-one consulting,

workshops, and training programs to help you evaluate your business idea and develop a plan for success.

3. Entrepreneurial Community Organizations: There are many entrepreneurial community organizations that offer free resources and support to aspiring entrepreneurs. These organizations often provide networking opportunities, mentorship, and educational resources. Examples include Startup Grind, Founder Institute, and Women Who Code.

4. Online Forums and Communities: There are many online forums and communities where entrepreneurs can share ideas, ask questions, and get feedback on their business ideas. Examples include Reddit's Entrepreneur subreddit, Quora, and LinkedIn Groups.

5. Business Planning Tools: There are many free online tools that can help you develop a business plan and evaluate the potential success of your business idea. Examples include LivePlan, Business Plan Pro, and Enloop.

6. Business Model Canvas: The Business Model Canvas is a strategic management tool that helps entrepreneurs and business owners to visualize and evaluate the key components of their business model. It is a one-page framework that outlines nine building blocks of a business, including customer segments, value proposition, channels, customer relationships, revenue streams, key resources, key activities, key partners, and cost structure. The canvas is designed to be flexible and adaptable to different types of businesses and can be used to identify areas for improvement, test new ideas, and communicate your business model to stakeholders. The canvas is available for

free online, and there are also many resources and templates available to help you use it effectively.

7. Lean Canvas: The Lean Canvas is a one-page business plan template that helps entrepreneurs quickly evaluate their business ideas by outlining key aspects such as customer segments, value proposition, key metrics, and more. You can find a free template and instructions on how to use it on the Lean Canvas website.

8. Value Proposition Canvas: The Value Proposition Canvas is a visual tool that helps you design and evaluate your value proposition by mapping out your customers' needs and how your product or service meets those needs. You can find a free template and instructions on how to use it on the Strategyzer website.

9. SWOT Analysis: A SWOT (Strengths, Weaknesses, Opportunities, Threats) Analysis is a framework for evaluating the internal and external factors that can impact the success of your business idea. You can use a free SWOT Analysis template to help identify key areas of strength, weakness, opportunity, and threat.

10. Business Plan Pitch Deck: A pitch deck is a presentation that provides an overview of your business idea, including your value proposition, target market, revenue model, and more. It can be a useful tool for pitching your idea to investors or potential partners. You can find free pitch deck templates and examples online.

11. Business Idea Evaluation Checklist: A business idea evaluation checklist can help you consider various factors such as market size, competition, scalability, and more to determine whether your business idea has the potential for success. You can find free checklists and templates online.

Here are some free resources related to artificial intelligence that can help you evaluate ideas before investing time and resources:

1. AI Business Canvas: Similar to the Business Model Canvas, the AI Business Canvas is a visual tool that helps you evaluate the feasibility of your AI idea by mapping out your business model, including your value proposition, target customers, data sources, algorithms, revenue streams, cost structure, and more. You can find a free template and instructions on how to use it on the AI Canvas website.

2. Kaggle: Kaggle is a platform that hosts data science and machine learning competitions and provides a wealth of datasets for exploration. You can use Kaggle to test your AI algorithms and evaluate their accuracy and performance. Additionally, Kaggle offers free courses on machine learning and data science.

3. TensorFlow: TensorFlow is an open-source platform for building and deploying machine learning models. It is widely used and supported by the AI community and provides a range of tools for developing and testing AI algorithms. TensorFlow offers free tutorials and courses on its website.

4. AI Ethics Guidelines: When working on an AI idea, it's important to consider the ethical implications of your technology. Several organizations, including the IEEE and the Partnership on AI, have developed guidelines and frameworks for responsible AI development. You can access these resources for free on their websites.

5. AI Startup Accelerators: Similar to startup accelerators, there are also AI-focused accelerators that provide resources and support to help entrepreneurs develop and evaluate their AI ideas. Some examples include Element AI and the Allen Institute for AI. These programs often provide mentorship, funding, and access to data and computing resources.

Evaluating the potential success of a business idea requires careful analysis and consideration of a range of factors. While it can be tempting to dive headfirst into a new venture, taking the time to evaluate the potential success of the idea can help avoid costly mistakes and improve the chances of success.

By conducting thorough market research, evaluating profitability and scalability, assessing feasibility and market timing, and considering potential risks and challenges, entrepreneurs can make informed decisions and pursue business ideas that have a greater likelihood of success. Overall, these resources can help you evaluate your AI idea from different angles and make informed decisions about whether to pursue it.

Chapter 2

Harnessing AI for Market Analysis, Forecasting, & Risk Assessment

As an entrepreneur, you know that market analysis, forecasting, and risk assessment are essential for the success of your business. But with limited resources and time, it can be challenging to conduct thorough research and make informed decisions. This is where artificial intelligence (AI) technology can help.

AI can provide you with valuable insights and intelligence that would be impossible to uncover through traditional methods. For example, using natural language processing (NLP) algorithms, you can analyze customer feedback, social media posts, and reviews to understand customer sentiment towards your brand or product. This information can be used to tailor your marketing campaigns and improve customer engagement, which can increase your revenue and brand loyalty.

AI can also help you forecast demand and identify potential supply chain disruptions, which is crucial for inventory management and resource allocation. With machine learning algorithms that analyze real-time data, you can get accurate and timely forecasts that can help you make informed decisions about production and sales. This can help you optimize your operations, reduce costs, and maximize profits.

Risk assessment is another critical aspect of running a successful business. With AI, you can identify potential risks and take appropriate measures to mitigate them. Fraud detection algorithms can analyze financial transactions to identify suspicious activity and prevent financial loss. AI can also analyze customer data and predict potential churn or identify customers who are most likely to purchase additional products or services.

While there are challenges to implementing AI, such as the quality and quantity of data required to train AI algorithms and the need for expertise in data science and AI, the benefits of AI are significant. AI can help you make data-driven decisions, reduce costs, improve customer satisfaction, and gain a competitive advantage.

I know what you're thinking. That's great and all, but I'm just getting started. How can I do all that when I barely have a budget to get my idea started? Fortunately, there are many open-source AI tools and platforms available that are readily accessible to the average person.

One of the most popular open-source AI tools for market analysis is Python. Python is a programming language that can be used for data analysis, machine learning, and AI. With Python, you can analyze large datasets, create predictive models, and automate data processing tasks. There are many free resources and tutorials available online to help you learn Python and develop your AI skills.

Another popular open-source AI tool is Apache Spark. Apache Spark is a distributed computing framework that can be used for big data processing, machine learning, and AI. With Apache Spark, you can process large datasets in real-time, develop machine learning models, and perform complex data analysis tasks. There are many online courses and tutorials available to help you learn Apache Spark and develop your AI skills.

If you are looking for a platform that requires no coding, you can consider using IBM Watson Studio. IBM Watson Studio is a cloud-based platform that allows you to build, train, and deploy AI models without any coding. With IBM Watson Studio, you can analyze data, create predictive models, and deploy your models to production. The platform also includes many pre-built AI models and templates that you can use to get started quickly.

Finally, you can consider using open-source AI libraries such as TensorFlow or PyTorch. These libraries provide pre-built AI models and algorithms that you can use to analyze data, develop predictive models, and automate data processing tasks. There are many online tutorials and resources available to help you learn how to use these libraries.

There are many open-source AI tools and platforms available that can help you harness the power of AI for market analysis, forecasting, and risk assessment. With these tools, you can analyze large datasets, create predictive models, and automate data processing tasks without the need for expensive tools or specialized expertise.

Investing in AI can give you a significant advantage over your competition. By harnessing the power of AI, you can gain insights and intelligence that can help you make informed decisions, reduce costs, and optimize your operations. As AI continues to evolve, investing in your AI capabilities can help your business stay ahead of the competition and achieve long-term success.

Chapter 3 - Creating a Business Plan with AI

Chapter 3

The Significance of a Well-Written Business Plan

The significance of a well-written business plan cannot be overstated. A business plan is a written document that outlines the goals, strategies, and financial projections for a business. It serves as a roadmap for entrepreneurs, investors, and other stakeholders to understand the vision and direction of the business.

One of the primary advantages of a comprehensive business plan is that it enables entrepreneurs to clarify their concepts and establish their objectives. By putting their ideas and goals into writing, business owners can gain a better understanding of their enterprise, identify potential challenges, and spot opportunities.

In addition, a business plan can help entrepreneurs communicate their vision and objectives to investors, partners, and other stakeholders effectively. A well-organized plan can demonstrate the potential of the business and enable investors to understand the risks and opportunities involved.

Moreover, a business plan can help entrepreneurs make sound financial decisions. By providing financial projections, entrepreneurs can identify the amount of funding required, the sources of revenue, and the costs involved. This can help them make informed decisions regarding pricing, expenses, and investments.

Furthermore, a business plan can help entrepreneurs anticipate and mitigate potential risks. By identifying potential challenges and developing contingency plans, entrepreneurs can be better prepared to respond to unexpected events and minimize their impact on the business.

Another benefit of a business plan is that it helps entrepreneurs measure their progress and adjust their strategies accordingly. By setting milestones and tracking progress against them, entrepreneurs can identify areas where they need to adjust or pivot their strategies.

In addition, a business plan can help entrepreneurs attract and retain talent. By outlining the mission, vision, and values of the business, entrepreneurs can attract employees who share their vision and are passionate about their work. This can create a strong and cohesive team that is committed to the success of the business.

Finally, a business plan can help entrepreneurs maintain focus and discipline. By outlining the goals and strategies of the business, entrepreneurs can stay focused on what is important and avoid distractions. This can help them stay on track and achieve their objectives.

A well-written business plan is a crucial document for any entrepreneur. It can help clarify ideas, communicate vision, manage finances, mitigate risks, measure progress, attract talent, and maintain focus. With a comprehensive plan, entrepreneurs can increase their chances of success and achieve their objectives.

Chapter 3

How can AI Assist in Creating a Business Plan, Identify Financial Projections, & Conduct Market Analysis?

In today's fast-paced business world, entrepreneurs and business owners need to be able to adapt quickly to changing market conditions and customer demands. One of the most critical aspects of building a successful business is creating a solid business plan that outlines your goals, strategies, and financial projections. With the advent of artificial intelligence (AI), it's easier than ever to create a comprehensive business plan, identify financial projections, and conduct market analysis. Here are some ways AI can assist in these areas:

1. Automated Financial Analysis - AI tools can help analyze your financial data to identify trends, patterns, and opportunities for growth. By using AI algorithms to analyze your data, you can quickly and easily identify areas of your business that are performing well and those that need improvement.

2. Predictive Analytics - AI tools can use predictive analytics to forecast future trends in your industry and help you make data-driven decisions. By analyzing past data and current market conditions, these tools can help you identify potential risks and opportunities and adjust your business strategy accordingly.

3. Natural Language Processing - AI tools that use natural language processing can help you create a well-written business plan by providing suggestions for wording, grammar, and structure. These tools can also help you

identify and highlight key points in your plan to ensure that it is concise, informative, and compelling.

4. Market Analysis - AI tools can help you conduct market analysis by analyzing customer behavior and trends. By using AI algorithms to analyze social media and other online data sources, you can gain insights into customer preferences and behaviors, which can inform your marketing and sales strategies.

5. Competitor Analysis - AI tools can help you analyze your competitors' strategies, products, and services to identify gaps in the market and potential areas for growth. By using AI algorithms to analyze competitor data, you can quickly identify areas of strength and weakness and adjust your business strategy accordingly.

6. Risk Assessment - AI tools can help you assess potential risks to your business by analyzing data from a range of sources, including financial records, market trends, and customer behavior. By using AI algorithms to identify potential risks, you can develop contingency plans to mitigate those risks and ensure the long-term success of your business.

7. Personalized Marketing - AI tools can help you create personalized marketing campaigns by analyzing customer data and tailoring your messaging to individual preferences and behaviors. By using AI algorithms to analyze customer behavior, you can identify opportunities for personalized marketing and adjust your messaging accordingly.

8. Financial Modeling - AI tools can help you create financial models that take into account a range of variables, including market trends, customer behavior, and

operational costs. By using AI algorithms to create financial models, you can identify potential revenue streams and develop strategies to maximize profitability.

9. Improved Decision Making - By using AI tools to analyze data and conduct market research, you can make more informed decisions about your business strategy, marketing campaigns, and financial projections. This can help you to optimize your business operations, improve profitability, and stay ahead of the competition.

There are many free, open-source tools available that can help you create a business plan, identify financial projections, and conduct market analysis using AI. These tools provide a wide range of features and functionality, so it's worth taking some time to explore them and find the ones that best meet your needs. Here are some of the more popular ones that can assist you in accomplishing the above tasks:

1. TensorFlow: TensorFlow is an open-source machine learning framework that can be used for a variety of tasks, including data analysis and market research. It provides a range of tools and libraries for building and training machine learning models that can be used to analyze market trends and make predictions about future market behavior.

2. R: R is a free, open-source programming language that is widely used for statistical analysis and data visualization. It provides a range of tools and libraries for data analysis, including data cleaning and preparation, statistical modeling, and visualization.

3. Python: Python is another popular programming language that can be used for data analysis and machine learning. It

has a large and active community of developers who have created a wide range of libraries and tools for data analysis, including NumPy, Pandas, and Scikit-learn.

4. Jupyter Notebook: Jupyter Notebook is an open-source web application that allows you to create and share documents that contain live code, equations, visualizations, and narrative text. It is a great tool for data analysis and modeling, as it allows you to run code snippets and view the results in real-time.

5. Apache Hadoop: Apache Hadoop is an open-source framework for distributed storage and processing of large data sets. It can be used to analyze large data sets and extract insights that can be used for market research and forecasting.

6. Apache Spark: Apache Spark is another open-source framework for distributed processing of large data sets. It is designed to be fast and efficient, making it a great tool for data analysis and machine learning.

7. OpenAI: OpenAI is a research organization dedicated to advancing artificial intelligence in a responsible and ethical manner. They have created a range of tools and libraries for natural language processing, machine learning, and other AI-related tasks.

8. Scrapy: Scrapy is an open-source web crawling framework that allows you to extract data from websites and APIs. It can be used to gather market research data and other information that can be used to inform business decisions.

9. Business Model Canvas - A free tool that allows you to create a visual representation of your business model.

10. Lean Canvas - A free tool that helps you to create a one-page business plan.
11. Enloop - A free business planning tool that uses AI to help you create financial projections, market analysis, and identify potential risks.
12. Canva - A free graphic design platform that allows you to create professional and visually appealing business plans.
13. HubSpot - A free marketing and sales software that includes tools for market analysis, customer segmentation, and competitive analysis.
14. Google Trends - A free tool that allows you to analyze search trends and identify market opportunities.
15. LivePlan - A cloud-based business planning tool that uses AI to help you create professional and effective business plans.
16. StratPad - A business planning software that uses AI to help you create a comprehensive business plan.
17. Bizplan - A business planning tool that uses AI to help you create professional and effective business plans.
18. IdeaBuddy - An AI-powered business planning tool that offers step-by-step guidance and enables you to create a comprehensive business plan.
19. Trello - A free project management tool that can help you keep track of your business plan development process and monitor progress.
20. MarketWatch - A website that provides free market news and analysis to help you stay informed on industry trends.

The use of AI can be a powerful tool for creating a comprehensive business plan, identifying financial projections, and conducting market analysis. By leveraging AI algorithms and tools, entrepreneurs and business owners can gain insights into customer behavior, market trends, and competitor strategies, allowing them to make more informed decisions about their business strategy and operations.

With the ever-increasing availability of AI tools and resources, there has never been a better time to harness the power of AI for your business.

Chapter 3

Case Studies: Using AI for Business Planning

As the use of artificial intelligence (AI) becomes more prevalent in various industries, it has proven to be a valuable tool for small to mid-sized businesses. One area where AI has shown great promise is in business planning, financial projections, and market analysis. In this section, we will explore five case studies of successful small to mid-sized businesses that have utilized AI to improve their operations in these areas. From data services to financial technology, these companies have demonstrated the power of AI in transforming their businesses and achieving success.

1. Appen: Appen is a data services and technology company that helps organizations improve their AI systems by providing them with high-quality training data. Appen used AI to streamline their data processing and analysis, which allowed them to provide their clients with faster, more accurate results. With the help of AI, Appen has grown from a small startup to a successful mid-sized business that operates in over 130 countries.

2. Brex: Brex is a financial technology company that offers corporate credit cards to startups and small businesses. Brex uses AI to analyze data from their customers' financial accounts, which allows them to make more informed decisions about credit limits and approvals. With the help of AI, Brex has been able to provide its customers with more flexible financing options and has grown into a successful business that has raised over $1 billion in funding.

3. Brighterion: Brighterion is a company that specializes in fraud prevention and identity verification. They use AI to analyze large amounts of data and identify potential fraudulent transactions. By using AI, Brighterion has been able to reduce the number of false positives and has helped its clients save millions of dollars in losses.

4. Kensho: Kensho is a financial technology company that uses AI to analyze financial data and provide insights to its clients. Kensho's AI platform can analyze massive amounts of data and identify patterns that humans may not be able to see. With the help of AI, Kensho has been able to provide its clients with valuable insights and has grown into a successful business that was acquired by S&P Global for $550 million.

5. SalesPredict: SalesPredict is a company that helps businesses improve their sales forecasting and lead generation by using AI. SalesPredict's AI platform can analyze customer data and predict which leads are most likely to convert into sales. With the help of AI, SalesPredict has been able to help its clients increase their sales and has grown into a successful business that was acquired by eBay for an undisclosed amount.

6. Hopper - Hopper is a travel app that leverages AI to help users find the best deals on flights and hotels. The app analyzes billions of data points to predict future prices and send notifications to users when it's the best time to book. This technology has helped Hopper achieve a 10x growth rate, reaching 30 million downloads and $1 billion in sales in just four years. The company has also raised $184 million in funding and was named one of Fast Company's Most Innovative Companies in 2018.

7. Blue River Technology - Blue River Technology is a precision agriculture company that uses computer vision and machine learning to help farmers optimize crop yields and reduce costs. Their AI-powered system, called See & Spray, identifies individual plants and applies herbicides only where necessary, reducing chemical usage by up to 90%. The company was acquired by John Deere in 2017 for $305 million and has been widely recognized for its innovative use of AI in agriculture.

8. Ocado - Ocado is a UK-based online supermarket that uses AI to manage inventory, optimize delivery routes, and improve customer service. The company's AI-powered robots can pick and pack an order of 50 items in just five minutes, reducing the time and cost of order fulfillment. Ocado has also partnered with other retailers to provide its AI-powered logistics services, generating additional revenue streams. The company's innovative use of AI has helped it become one of the largest online grocery retailers in the world, with a market capitalization of over £20 billion.

9. Grammarly - Grammarly is a writing assistant tool that uses AI to help users improve their writing. The tool checks for spelling and grammar errors, offers suggestions for word choice and sentence structure, and provides feedback on tone and style. Grammarly has over 20 million daily active users and has raised $200 million in funding. The company has also expanded its AI-powered writing assistant to other applications, including Microsoft Office and Google Docs.

10. Freenome - Freenome is a biotech company that uses AI to detect early-stage cancer. The company's AI-powered

platform analyzes blood samples for tiny fragments of cancer DNA, allowing for earlier detection and treatment. Freenome has raised over $500 million in funding and has partnerships with several major pharmaceutical companies. The company's innovative use of AI in cancer detection has the potential to save millions of lives and revolutionize the field of oncology.

These case studies demonstrate that AI can be a game-changer for small to mid-sized businesses, providing valuable insights and solutions for planning, financial forecasting, and market analysis. With the increasing availability and affordability of AI tools and platforms, businesses of all sizes can now leverage these technologies to gain a competitive edge. By harnessing the power of AI, businesses can make better decisions, improve efficiency, and ultimately achieve their goals. As AI continues to evolve and become more accessible, it will undoubtedly continue to transform the way businesses operate and compete in the marketplace.

Chapter 4 - Challenges & Limitations of AI in Business Planning

Chapter 4

Potential Issues with AI-Generated Business Ideas & Plans

Artificial intelligence has come a long way in the past few years, and its impact on the business world cannot be overstated. AI-generated business ideas and plans can be incredibly useful, as they can help entrepreneurs and business owners quickly evaluate and identify potential opportunities. However, there are also potential issues that come with using AI-generated business ideas and plans, and it is important to be aware of these issues before relying too heavily on AI-generated solutions.

One of the primary concerns with using AI-generated business ideas and plans is the lack of human creativity and intuition. While AI is incredibly advanced, it is still a machine and does not possess the same level of creativity and intuition as humans. This means that AI-generated business ideas and plans may be limited in their scope and may not consider certain factors that are important to humans, such as emotions, social dynamics, and cultural nuances.

Another issue with AI-generated business ideas and plans is the potential for bias. AI algorithms are only as unbiased as the data they are trained on, and if the data contains biases or inaccuracies, the resulting business ideas and plans will also contain biases and inaccuracies. This can be particularly problematic if the biases are related to issues such as race, gender, or socio-economic status.

An additional potential issue with AI-generated business ideas and plans is the lack of context. AI algorithms can only make decisions based on the data they have been trained on, and if the data does not provide enough context, the resulting business ideas and plans may not be relevant or useful. This can be particularly problematic in industries where there is a lot of nuance and complexity, such as healthcare or education.

A concern with AI-generated business ideas and plans is the potential for overreliance on technology. While AI can be incredibly useful, it should never be a substitute for human decision-making. Human judgement is still critical in evaluating the potential success of a business idea or plan, and it is important to use AI-generated solutions as one tool among many.

There is also the potential for data privacy issues when using AI-generated business ideas and plans. AI algorithms require large amounts of data to be trained on, and if this data is not properly secured, it can be vulnerable to hacking or other forms of unauthorized access. This can be particularly problematic if the data contains sensitive information about individuals or organizations.

Furthermore, there is also a lack of transparency in AI-generated business ideas and plans. It can be difficult to understand how an AI algorithm arrived at a certain recommendation or decision, which can make it challenging to evaluate the accuracy and reliability of the recommendations. This lack of transparency can also make it difficult to address any biases or inaccuracies in the algorithm.

Finally, there is also the issue of accountability when using AI-generated business ideas and plans. If a business decision based on an AI-generated plan goes wrong, it can be difficult to assign responsibility or liability. This can be particularly problematic in industries where there are legal or regulatory requirements that need to be met.

While AI-generated business ideas and plans can be incredibly useful, there are also potential issues that need to be considered. It is important to be aware of these issues and to use AI-generated solutions as one tool among many in the decision-making process. By doing so, businesses can take advantage of the benefits of AI while also minimizing the potential risks.

Chapter 4

Limitations of AI and the Need for Human Input & Expertise

Artificial intelligence (AI) has revolutionized the way we do business, from automating routine tasks to developing sophisticated predictive models. However, despite the many benefits of AI, there are still significant limitations to what it can achieve. Specifically, there is a critical need for human input and expertise in business operations that cannot be replaced by AI alone.

One of the main limitations of AI is that it is only as good as the data it is trained on. If the data is biased, incomplete, or otherwise flawed, the AI will produce similarly flawed results. For example, an AI system that is trained on historical data that is biased against certain groups may produce similarly biased results when used to make predictions about those groups in the future. This highlights the importance of human oversight and input in ensuring that the data used to train AI systems is accurate, unbiased, and representative.

Another limitation of AI is that it is not capable of understanding the nuances of human behavior and decision-making. AI can certainly analyze data and make predictions based on that data, but it cannot replicate the complex thought processes and reasoning that humans use to make decisions. This means that AI-generated business ideas and plans may lack the strategic insights and creativity that only humans can provide.

AI-generated business ideas and plans may lack the ability to incorporate ethical considerations and social responsibility. AI is only concerned with maximizing efficiency and profitability, but businesses must also consider their impact on society and the environment. This is where human input and expertise become essential in ensuring that businesses operate in a responsible and sustainable manner.

Another challenge with AI-generated business ideas and plans is the lack of context and intuition. While AI is excellent at analyzing data and patterns, it lacks the context and intuition that humans bring to decision-making. For example, an AI system may identify a potential market opportunity based on data analysis but may miss crucial factors such as cultural differences, market trends, and consumer behavior. This is where human input and expertise are critical in ensuring that business decisions are made with the full context and intuition necessary for success.

Another limitation of AI is its inability to replicate the personal touch and empathy that is essential in many business interactions. AI-generated business plans may lack the ability to build relationships with customers, suppliers, and employees, and may fail to consider the emotional and psychological factors that influence business decisions. This is where human input and expertise become crucial in ensuring that businesses can build strong relationships and provide personalized services that meet the needs of their customers and employees.

Finally, AI-generated business ideas and plans may lack the ability to adapt to changing circumstances and unforeseen events. While AI is excellent at analyzing data and making predictions, it is not as adept at adapting to unexpected changes in the business environment. This is where human input and expertise become essential in ensuring that businesses can navigate challenges and take advantage of new opportunities as they arise.

While AI has tremendous potential to transform the way we do business, it is not a panacea for all business challenges. The limitations of AI highlight the need for human input and expertise in ensuring that businesses operate ethically, sustainably, and successfully. Businesses must strive to strike the right balance between AI-generated insights and human intuition, creativity, and empathy to achieve long-term success in today's rapidly changing business environment.

Chapter 5 - Best Practices for Integrating AI into Business Planning

Chapter 5

Incorporating AI into Business Planning Processes

Artificial Intelligence (AI) has become an essential tool in modern business planning processes. With AI, businesses can perform complex data analyses, create accurate financial projections, and identify market trends that can help guide their decision-making. However, incorporating AI into your business planning process can be a daunting task. It's not just about buying the latest AI software or hiring the best data scientists.

To effectively incorporate AI into your business planning processes, you need a well-thought-out strategy that considers your business needs, available resources, and existing processes. Here are some tips for effectively incorporating AI into your business planning processes.

1. Identify Business Goals and Needs: Before incorporating AI into your business planning processes, you need to identify your business goals and needs. This involves understanding what your business wants to achieve, its strengths and weaknesses, and the gaps that AI can fill. For instance, you may want to improve your business forecasting, optimize your supply chain, or identify new markets. Once you have identified your goals and needs, you can start looking for AI solutions that fit your requirements.

2. Evaluate Available Resources: Incorporating AI into your business planning processes requires the right resources. You need to evaluate the available resources to determine if they are sufficient for the task at hand. This involves

assessing your budget, IT infrastructure, and human resources. For instance, you may need to invest in new hardware or software, hire data scientists, or upskill your existing staff.

3. Choose the Right AI Tools: Choosing the right AI tools is crucial to the success of your business planning processes. The AI tools you choose should align with your business goals and needs. There are several AI tools available in the market, each with its strengths and weaknesses. Some of the popular AI tools for business planning include machine learning algorithms, natural language processing, and predictive analytics. You need to evaluate each tool's capabilities and limitations and choose the ones that best fit your business requirements.

4. Integrate AI with Existing Processes: To effectively incorporate AI into your business planning processes, you need to integrate it with your existing processes. This involves understanding how AI fits into your current workflows and how it can enhance them. For instance, you can integrate AI into your financial planning processes to create more accurate financial projections or integrate AI into your supply chain to optimize inventory management.

5. Collect and Manage Quality Data: AI relies on data to make accurate predictions and recommendations. Therefore, it's crucial to collect and manage quality data to effectively incorporate AI into your business planning processes. This involves collecting data from various sources, cleaning and organizing it, and ensuring its quality. You also need to establish data governance policies and procedures to ensure data security, privacy, and compliance.

6. Train Your AI Models: To make accurate predictions and recommendations, your AI models need to be trained on relevant data. Therefore, you need to invest in data training to effectively incorporate AI into your business planning processes. This involves providing your AI models with the right data sets, ensuring they are labeled correctly, and validating their accuracy.

7. Test and Validate Your AI Models: Testing and validating your AI models is crucial to ensure they are accurate and reliable. This involves running multiple tests on your AI models, comparing their performance to the expected outcomes, and validating their accuracy. You also need to establish metrics to measure the success of your AI models.

8. Monitor and Refine Your AI Models: AI models require constant monitoring and refinement to ensure they remain accurate and reliable. Therefore, you need to establish a monitoring and refinement process to effectively incorporate AI into your business planning processes. This involves monitoring the performance of your AI models, identifying any errors or inconsistencies, and refining them to improve their accuracy.

9. Combine human expertise with AI: While AI can automate many business planning processes, it is still essential to combine it with human expertise. Human input can provide context and help identify potential biases in the data or models. Combining human expertise with AI can provide more accurate and reliable results.

10. Plan for scalability: Implementing AI in business planning processes should be scalable. Consider the potential growth of your business and the scalability of the AI tools

used. Ensure that the tools can handle large volumes of data and can be easily integrated into other systems.

11. Ensure compliance with regulations: AI-generated insights and predictions must comply with industry regulations and ethical standards. Ensure that the data inputs and AI models used are compliant with relevant regulations and ethical standards.

While AI has tremendous potential to transform the way we do business, it is not a panacea for all business challenges. The limitations of AI highlight the need for human input and expertise in ensuring that businesses operate ethically, sustainably, and successfully. Businesses must strive to strike the right balance between AI-generated insights and human intuition, creativity, and empathy to achieve long-term success in today's rapidly changing business environment.

Chapter 5

Common Challenges & Limitations of AI

Artificial intelligence (AI) has become a popular tool for businesses to improve their planning processes, but it also comes with its own set of challenges and limitations. In this section, we will explore some strategies for overcoming common challenges and limitations of AI in business planning.

1. Understand the limitations of AI: AI is not a magic solution and has its own set of limitations. It is important to understand these limitations to set realistic expectations for what AI can achieve. For instance, AI may not always be able to accurately predict human behavior or emotions.

2. Combine AI with human expertise: To overcome the limitations of AI, it is important to combine AI with human expertise. Human input can help provide context, interpret results, and make informed decisions based on AI-generated insights.

3. Choose the right data: AI relies heavily on data to generate insights and predictions. Choosing the right data is crucial to ensure that the AI-generated insights are accurate and reliable.

4. Ensure data quality: The accuracy and reliability of AI-generated insights are only as good as the data that is fed into the AI algorithm. It is important to ensure that the data is clean, accurate, and relevant.

5. Keep the business goals in mind: AI-generated insights and recommendations should always be aligned with the business goals. It is important to ensure that the AI-generated insights and recommendations are relevant to the business and can help achieve the desired outcomes.

6. Regularly review and update AI algorithms: AI algorithms are not set in stone and can be updated and improved over time. It is important to regularly review and update AI algorithms to ensure that they are providing accurate and relevant insights.

7. Consider the ethical implications of AI: AI can also have ethical implications, and it is important to consider these implications when using AI in business planning. For instance, AI-generated insights may be biased or discriminatory, and it is important to ensure that the AI algorithms are fair and unbiased.

8. Test and validate AI-generated insights: Before making any decisions based on AI-generated insights, it is important to test and validate these insights. This can help ensure that the insights are accurate and reliable and can help reduce the risk of making incorrect decisions based on flawed insights.

9. Use AI as a tool, not a replacement: It is important to remember that AI is a tool and not a replacement for human expertise. While AI can provide valuable insights and predictions, it is important to combine these insights with human expertise to make informed decisions.

10. Train employees to work with AI: AI can be a complex and intimidating technology for employees who are not familiar with it. It is important to provide training to employees on how to work with AI-generated insights and recommendations to ensure that they can effectively use these insights in their work.

AI can be a powerful tool for businesses to improve their planning processes. However, it is important to understand the limitations and challenges of AI and to develop strategies for overcoming these challenges.

By combining AI with human expertise, choosing the right data, ensuring data quality, and keeping the business goals in mind, businesses can effectively incorporate AI into their planning processes and make informed decisions based on accurate and reliable insights.

Chapter 5

Successful Implementations of AI in Business Planning & Ideation

Artificial Intelligence (AI) is revolutionizing the way businesses operate across all sectors. The ability to gather, process and analyze vast amounts of data has led to the development of new tools and approaches that are transforming the business world. From financial forecasting to market analysis, AI is playing an increasingly important role in business planning and ideation. In this section, we will explore some of the most successful implementations of AI in business planning and ideation.

1. IBM Watson: IBM Watson is one of the most successful examples of AI in business planning. The Watson platform uses natural language processing and machine learning to help businesses make better decisions. It can analyze large amounts of data and provide insights that would be impossible for humans to find on their own. For example, Watson can help businesses identify potential risks and opportunities in the market and provide recommendations on how to mitigate those risks or take advantage of those opportunities.

2. Amazon: Amazon has been using AI in its business planning for many years, and it is one of the most successful companies in the world. The company uses AI to optimize its supply chain, personalize customer experiences, and even develop new products. For example, Amazon's recommendation engine uses machine learning to analyze customer data and provide

personalized product recommendations. This has helped the company increase sales and improve customer loyalty.

3. Google: Google has been using AI in its business planning for many years, and it is one of the most successful companies in the world. The company uses AI to optimize its search algorithms, personalize user experiences, and even develop new products. For example, Google's search engine uses machine learning to analyze user data and provide personalized search results. This has helped the company maintain its dominance in the search engine market.

4. Airbnb: Airbnb is a leading player in the sharing economy, and it has been using AI in its business planning for many years. The company uses AI to optimize its pricing algorithms, personalize guest experiences, and even predict demand. For example, Airbnb's pricing algorithm uses machine learning to analyze market data and provide personalized pricing recommendations. This has helped the company increase its revenue and improve its profitability.

5. Netflix: Netflix is a leading player in the streaming video market, and it has been using AI in its business planning for many years. The company uses AI to personalize its user experience, optimize its content recommendations, and even develop new shows. For example, Netflix's recommendation engine uses machine learning to analyze user data and provide personalized content recommendations. This has helped the company maintain its position as a leader in the streaming video market.

AI is playing an increasingly important role in business planning and ideation. These examples demonstrate how companies can leverage AI to gain a competitive edge, improve decision-making, and ultimately achieve their goals. By incorporating AI into their business planning processes, companies can stay ahead of the curve and drive growth in the rapidly changing business landscape.

Chapter 6 - Future Trends in AI & Business Planning

Chapter 6

Emerging Technologies & Innovation

Artificial Intelligence (AI) has revolutionized the way businesses operate, providing numerous benefits such as increased efficiency, improved decision-making, and enhanced customer experiences. In the field of business planning, AI has proven to be a valuable tool, helping businesses to make better decisions and develop more accurate financial projections.

As the technology continues to evolve, new innovations are emerging that are likely to have a significant impact on AI-driven business planning. In this section, we will discuss some of the emerging technologies and innovations that are likely to shape the future of AI-driven business planning.

1. Machine Learning: Machine learning is a subset of AI that involves the development of algorithms that can learn from data and improve their performance over time. In the context of business planning, machine learning algorithms can be used to analyze large data sets and identify patterns and trends that may not be immediately apparent to human analysts. This can be particularly useful in areas such as market analysis, where large volumes of data need to be processed quickly to make informed decisions.

2. Natural Language Processing: Natural Language Processing (NLP) is a subfield of AI that focuses on the interaction between computers and human language. With NLP, businesses can use machine learning algorithms to analyze text data and extract meaningful insights. This can

be particularly useful for businesses that rely heavily on customer feedback or social media data to make decisions.

3. Predictive Analytics: Predictive analytics involves using statistical algorithms and machine learning techniques to analyze historical data and make predictions about future events. In the context of business planning, predictive analytics can be used to forecast future trends and identify potential risks and opportunities. This can be particularly useful in industries where the future is difficult to predict, such as finance and healthcare.

4. Blockchain Technology: Blockchain technology is a decentralized ledger system that allows multiple parties to record transactions in a secure and transparent manner. In the context of business planning, blockchain technology can be used to securely store and share sensitive information between parties, such as financial projections and market research data. This can help to increase transparency and trust between parties, leading to more effective decision-making.

5. Cloud Computing: Cloud computing involves using a network of remote servers to store, manage, and process data. In the context of business planning, cloud computing can be used to store large data sets and run complex AI algorithms. This can be particularly useful for small businesses that may not have the resources to invest in expensive hardware or software.

6. Robotic Process Automation: Robotic Process Automation (RPA) involves using software robots to automate repetitive tasks, such as data entry and report generation. In the context of business planning, RPA can be used to automate tasks such as financial analysis and

report generation, freeing up employees to focus on more strategic tasks.

7. Virtual and Augmented Reality: Virtual and Augmented Reality (VR/AR) technologies allow users to experience a computer-generated environment in a realistic way. In the context of business planning, VR/AR technologies can be used to simulate different business scenarios and test the impact of different decisions in a virtual environment. This can help businesses to make more informed decisions and minimize the risk of costly mistakes.

8. Quantum Computing: Quantum computing is an emerging technology that involves using quantum-mechanical phenomena to perform computations. In the context of business planning, quantum computing can be used to perform complex calculations that are currently beyond the capabilities of traditional computers. This can help businesses to develop more accurate financial projections and make more informed decisions.

The field of AI-driven business planning is rapidly evolving, with new technologies and innovations emerging all the time. As businesses increasingly turn to AI to gain a competitive edge, it is important to stay up to date on the latest developments and trends. By understanding the potential benefits and limitations of AI, and by adopting strategies to overcome common challenges, businesses can effectively leverage this technology to create more accurate, efficient, and data-driven business plans. As we look to the future, AI will continue to play a critical role in shaping the way businesses operate and compete in the marketplace.

Chapter 6

Insights from Industry Experts on AI's Evolution

As the field of artificial intelligence continues to rapidly evolve, industry experts are weighing in on how it is likely to impact business planning and ideation in the coming years. One key insight is that AI is likely to become even more sophisticated and capable, allowing businesses to gain even deeper insights into their customers and markets. This will enable them to make more informed decisions and take advantage of new opportunities as they arise.

"We're still in the early days of AI, and we're going to see a lot of evolution in the next few years. The biggest advancements are going to come from the application of AI in new areas, like healthcare and education, and from the development of new technologies that can learn from less data and require less supervision." - Andrew Ng, founder of Google Brain and former chief scientist at Baidu.

Another important trend to watch is the rise of explainable AI. This refers to AI systems that are designed to provide clear and transparent explanations of their decision-making processes, making it easier for humans to understand and interpret the results. This is important because it will help to build trust and confidence in AI systems, which will be crucial as they become increasingly integrated into business planning processes.

"The key to advancing AI is to focus on creating systems that are explainable and transparent. This will help to build trust between humans and machines and ensure that AI is being used in a responsible and ethical way." - Yoshua Bengio, co-recipient of the 2018 Turing Award.

Many experts also predict that AI will become increasingly integrated with other emerging technologies, such as blockchain and the Internet of Things (IoT). This will enable businesses to gather and analyze vast amounts of data from a wide range of sources, providing them with even deeper insights into their operations and markets. It will also enable them to automate many routine tasks and processes, freeing up human employees to focus on more strategic work.

In addition, there is likely to be a continued trend towards AI platforms and tools that are designed specifically for business planning and ideation. These platforms will be highly customizable and modular, allowing businesses to easily integrate them into their existing workflows and processes. They will also be highly user-friendly, making it easy for non-technical users to leverage the power of AI in their work.

"The next phase of AI will be about creating systems that can reason and make decisions in the same way that humans do. This will require us to develop AI that can understand context, reason logically, and make ethical judgments." - Demis Hassabis, co-founder and CEO of DeepMind.

Finally, experts predict that there will be continued growth in the use of AI-powered chatbots and virtual assistants for customer service and support. These systems will become increasingly sophisticated, allowing them to handle more complex tasks and interactions with customers. They will also become more personalized and context-aware, providing customers with a highly tailored and intuitive experience.

Overall, the future of AI in business planning and ideation is likely to be characterized by increasing sophistication, integration with other emerging technologies, and a focus on explainability and transparency. As these trends continue to evolve, it will be important for businesses to stay up to date with the latest developments to take full advantage of the benefits that AI can provide. By doing so, they will be better positioned to compete and succeed in the fast-paced and ever-changing business landscape of the future.

Chapter 6

Staying Ahead of the Curve

Artificial Intelligence (AI) is transforming the business landscape at a rapid pace. As the technology continues to evolve, companies that fail to leverage its power for planning and innovation risk falling behind their competitors. In this section, we explore twelve predictions for how businesses can stay ahead of the curve in leveraging AI, from building a data-driven culture to prioritizing ethical AI. By embracing these strategies, businesses can unlock the full potential of AI and gain a competitive advantage in today's fast-paced business world.

1. Understand Your Business Needs: AI can help businesses in many ways, but the technology is not a silver bullet that can solve all problems. The first step to staying ahead of the curve is to understand your business needs and identify areas where AI can add value.

2. Identify Opportunities for Automation: One of the most significant benefits of AI is automation. Companies can use AI to automate routine tasks and free up human resources for more strategic work. Identify opportunities for automation, such as data entry, customer service, and supply chain management, to improve efficiency and productivity.

3. Build a Data-Driven Culture: AI requires data, and lots of it. Businesses that want to leverage AI for planning and innovation need to build a data-driven culture. This means collecting and analyzing data from every part of the organization and using it to drive decision-making.

4. Invest in Data Infrastructure: To build a data-driven culture, businesses need to invest in data infrastructure. This includes data storage, processing, and analysis tools. Companies that can quickly access and analyze data will be better positioned to leverage AI for planning and innovation.

5. Develop AI Expertise: AI is a complex and rapidly evolving field. Businesses that want to leverage the technology need to develop AI expertise in-house. This can be done by hiring data scientists and AI experts, or by upskilling existing employees.

6. Leverage Cloud-Based AI Services: Developing AI expertise in-house can be time-consuming and expensive. Many cloud-based AI services, such as Amazon Web Services and Microsoft Azure, offer pre-built AI tools that businesses can leverage without extensive in-house expertise.

7. Foster Collaboration Between Humans and AI: AI is not a replacement for humans, but a tool that can help us work more effectively. Businesses that want to stay ahead of the curve in leveraging AI for planning and innovation need to foster collaboration between humans and AI. This means creating workflows that incorporate both human and AI decision-making.

8. Use AI to Augment Human Intelligence: AI can help humans make better decisions by providing insights and predictions based on large amounts of data. Businesses that want to stay ahead of the curve need to use AI to augment human intelligence, rather than replace it.

9. Monitor and Manage Bias: AI is only as unbiased as the data it is trained on. Businesses that want to leverage AI

for planning and innovation need to monitor and manage bias in their data and algorithms. This includes diversifying data sources, using diverse training datasets, and regularly auditing algorithms for bias.

10. Continuously Evaluate AI Performance: AI is not a set-it-and-forget-it technology. Businesses that want to stay ahead of the curve need to continuously evaluate AI performance and adjust algorithms as necessary. This includes monitoring accuracy, speed, and bias.

11. Stay Ahead of Regulatory Changes: As AI becomes more prevalent, governments around the world are introducing regulations to govern its use. Businesses that want to stay ahead of the curve need to stay abreast of regulatory changes and ensure they are following all applicable laws and regulations.

12. Prioritize Ethical AI: AI has the potential to do great good, but it also has the potential to do harm. Businesses that want to stay ahead of the curve in leveraging AI for planning and innovation need to prioritize ethical AI. This means developing and adhering to ethical principles for AI development and use.

By following the predictions outlined in this section, businesses can optimize their use of AI for planning and innovation, improve efficiency and productivity, and gain a competitive edge in their industries.

Through embracing a data-driven culture, investing in infrastructure, developing AI expertise, fostering collaboration between humans and AI, and prioritizing ethical AI, businesses can unlock the full potential of this transformative technology and position themselves for success in the years to come.

Chapter 7 - The Human Element: Balancing AI with Human Expertise

Chapter 7

Staying Ahead of the Curve

Artificial Intelligence (AI) has revolutionized the way businesses plan and innovate, but the role of human input and expertise cannot be understated. AI can analyze data and identify patterns, but it cannot replicate human intuition, creativity, and experience. In this section, we explore the critical role that human input and expertise play in AI-driven business planning and ideation. From understanding the limitations of AI to collaborating effectively between humans and machines, we outline strategies that businesses can use to optimize the synergy between humans and AI.

1. Humans Are Still Essential: AI is powerful, but it is not a substitute for human input and expertise. While AI can analyze data and make predictions, it cannot replicate human creativity, intuition, and experience. Humans are still essential in driving innovation and planning for the future.

2. AI Can Enhance Human Capabilities: While humans are still essential, AI can enhance human capabilities. AI can analyze vast amounts of data and identify patterns and insights that would be difficult for humans to uncover on their own. AI can also automate routine tasks, freeing up human resources for more strategic work.

3. Collaboration Is Key: The most effective use of AI in business planning and ideation is through collaboration between humans and AI. Humans can provide context and expertise to help AI make more informed predictions, and

AI can provide data-driven insights to support human decision-making.

4. Understand the Limitations of AI: AI is powerful, but it is not perfect. Understanding the limitations of AI is critical in ensuring that humans can provide the necessary input and expertise. AI can struggle with ambiguity, context, and subjective reasoning, making human input essential in these areas.

5. Ensure the Quality of Input Data: AI relies on data to provide insights and make predictions. Ensuring the quality of input data is critical in ensuring that AI can provide accurate and useful insights. Humans can help ensure the quality of input data by providing context and domain expertise.

6. Use AI to Identify Trends and Patterns: One of the most significant benefits of AI in business planning and ideation is its ability to identify trends and patterns in large datasets. This can provide insights that humans may have overlooked and help identify emerging opportunities and threats.

7. Use Human Expertise to Interpret AI Insights: While AI can identify trends and patterns, it is up to humans to interpret these insights and make strategic decisions. Human expertise is critical in ensuring that AI insights are relevant, accurate, and actionable.

8. Augment Human Creativity with AI: AI can be used to augment human creativity in business planning and ideation. By identifying patterns and providing insights, AI can help humans generate more creative and innovative ideas.

9. Use AI to Automate Routine Tasks: AI can be used to automate routine tasks in business planning and ideation, such as data entry and analysis. This can free up human resources for more strategic work and improve overall efficiency.

10. Prioritize Data Privacy and Security: AI relies on large amounts of data to provide insights and make predictions. However, ensuring data privacy and security is critical in ensuring that this data is used responsibly. Businesses that prioritize data privacy and security will be better positioned to leverage AI for business planning and ideation.

11. Continuously Monitor and Evaluate AI Performance: AI is not a set-it-and-forget-it technology. Continuously monitoring and evaluating AI performance is critical in ensuring that it is providing accurate and useful insights. This includes monitoring accuracy, speed, and bias.

12. Embrace an Agile Approach: AI-driven business planning and ideation require an agile approach. By embracing an agile approach, businesses can quickly adapt to new insights and emerging trends, ensuring that they remain competitive and innovative.

The role of human input and expertise in AI-driven business planning and ideation is crucial in ensuring that businesses remain competitive and innovative. By understanding the limitations of AI, collaborating effectively, ensuring data quality and security, continuously monitoring & evaluating AI performance, and embracing an agile approach, businesses can optimize the synergy between humans and machines.

By augmenting human creativity and expertise with AI insights, businesses can leverage the full potential of this transformative technology while still maintaining the unique perspective that only humans can provide. By recognizing the strengths of both humans and AI, businesses can drive innovation and planning to new heights.

Chapter 7

Integrating Human Perspectives & Insights into AI-Generated Plans & Ideas

Artificial Intelligence (AI) has transformed the way businesses plan and innovate. AI-generated plans and ideas can provide valuable insights and predictions, but it is crucial to integrate human perspectives and insights to ensure that the plans and ideas align with the business's goals and values. In this chapter, we explore strategies for effectively integrating human perspectives and insights into AI-generated plans and ideas.

1. Understand the Limitations of AI: The first step in effectively integrating human perspectives and insights into AI-generated plans and ideas is to understand the limitations of AI. While AI can provide valuable insights and predictions, it cannot replicate human intuition, creativity, and experience. Humans are still essential in driving innovation and ensuring that plans and ideas align with the business's goals and values.

2. Prioritize Human Input: To effectively integrate human perspectives and insights into AI-generated plans and ideas, it is essential to prioritize human input. Humans should be involved in every step of the planning process, from identifying the problem to generating ideas and evaluating solutions. By prioritizing human input, businesses can ensure that AI-generated plans and ideas align with their goals and values.

3. Establish Clear Goals and Values: To effectively integrate human perspectives and insights into AI-generated plans and ideas, businesses must establish clear goals and

values. Human input is critical in defining these goals and values, as they reflect the unique perspective and expertise of the business's stakeholders.

4. Ensure Diversity and Inclusion: To effectively integrate human perspectives and insights into AI-generated plans and ideas, businesses must ensure diversity and inclusion in the planning process. This includes ensuring representation from different departments, demographics, and perspectives. By ensuring diversity and inclusion, businesses can benefit from a range of perspectives and ideas.

5. Use AI to Identify Trends and Patterns: One of the most significant benefits of AI in business planning and ideation is its ability to identify trends and patterns in large datasets. This can provide insights that humans may have overlooked and help identify emerging opportunities and threats. By leveraging AI to identify trends and patterns, businesses can incorporate these insights into their plans and ideas.

6. Augment Human Creativity with AI: AI can be used to augment human creativity in business planning and ideation. By identifying patterns and providing insights, AI can help humans generate more creative and innovative ideas. This can help ensure that AI-generated plans and ideas align with the business's goals and values.

7. Use Human Expertise to Interpret AI Insights: While AI can identify trends and patterns, it is up to humans to interpret these insights and make strategic decisions. Human expertise is critical in ensuring that AI insights are relevant, accurate, and actionable. By leveraging human expertise to interpret AI insights, businesses can ensure

that AI-generated plans and ideas align with their goals and values.

8. Encourage Open Communication: To effectively integrate human perspectives and insights into AI-generated plans and ideas, businesses must encourage open communication. This includes creating a culture of transparency, where all stakeholders feel comfortable sharing their opinions and ideas. By encouraging open communication, businesses can benefit from a range of perspectives and ideas.

9. Use AI to Automate Routine Tasks: AI can be used to automate routine tasks in business planning and ideation, such as data entry and analysis. This can free up human resources for more strategic work and improve overall efficiency. By leveraging AI to automate routine tasks, businesses can ensure that human resources are used effectively.

10. Continuously Monitor and Evaluate AI Performance: AI is not a set-it-and-forget-it technology. Continuously monitoring and evaluating AI performance is critical in ensuring that it is providing accurate and useful insights. This includes monitoring accuracy, speed, and bias. By continuously monitoring and evaluating AI performance, businesses can ensure that AI-generated plans and ideas. By providing adequate training and support, businesses can ensure that employees are equipped with the knowledge and skills to effectively integrate human perspectives and insights into AI-generated plans and ideas.

11. Foster a Culture of Innovation: Finally, to effectively integrate human perspectives and insights into AI-

generated plans and ideas, businesses must foster a culture of innovation. This includes encouraging experimentation, taking risks, and learning from failures. By fostering a culture of innovation, businesses can ensure that AI-generated plans and ideas are not limited by preconceived notions or fear of failure. This can help businesses to stay ahead of the curve in leveraging AI for planning and innovation.

Integrating human perspectives and insights into AI-generated plans and ideas is crucial for businesses to stay ahead of the curve in leveraging AI for planning and innovation. By prioritizing human input, fostering diversity and inclusion, and using AI to augment human creativity and expertise, businesses can ensure that their AI-generated plans and ideas align with their goals and values.

It is important for businesses to continuously monitor and evaluate AI performance, provide adequate training, and support to employees, and foster a culture of innovation to remain competitive in today's rapidly evolving business landscape. By effectively integrating human perspectives and insights into AI-generated plans and ideas, businesses can unlock new opportunities for growth and success.

Chapter 7

Finding a Balance Between AI & Human Contributions

The integration of AI into business planning and ideation has the potential to revolutionize the way businesses operate. By harnessing the power of AI, businesses can gain valuable insights, identify patterns, and make more informed decisions. However, as with any new technology, there are considerations that must be considered to ensure that a balance is struck between AI and human contributions. In this chapter, we will explore key considerations for ensuring a balance between AI and human contributions to business planning and ideation.

To ensure a balance between AI and human contributions, it is important to define clear roles and responsibilities. This includes identifying which tasks will be automated with AI and which tasks will require human input. By defining clear roles and responsibilities, businesses can ensure that both AI and human contributions are utilized to their full potential.

While AI can provide valuable insights, it is necessary to prioritize human input. This includes utilizing human creativity, intuition, and experience to complement AI-generated insights. By prioritizing human input, businesses can ensure that AI-generated plans and ideas are grounded in real-world experience and expertise.

Fostering collaboration between AI and human teams is important to safeguard a balance between AI and human contributions. This includes encouraging open communication and knowledge sharing between AI and human teams. By fostering collaboration, businesses can ensure that both AI and human contributions are utilized to their full potential.

Ensuring diversity and inclusion is another critical consideration for balancing AI and human contributions. By incorporating diverse perspectives and experiences, businesses can ensure that AI-generated plans and ideas are not limited by a narrow worldview. This can lead to more innovative and inclusive solutions.

Using AI to automate routine tasks is one way to find a balance between AI and human contributions. This frees up time and resources for humans to focus on higher-level tasks that require creativity and critical thinking. By automating routine tasks, businesses can ensure that both AI and human contributions are utilized efficiently.

While AI can provide valuable insights, it is important to remember that creativity is a uniquely human trait. To ensure a balance between AI and human contributions, businesses should consider using AI to augment human creativity. This includes using AI to identify patterns and trends that humans may not have otherwise noticed.

Although AI can provide crucial insights, it is crucial to leverage human expertise in interpreting these insights. This involves employing human knowledge to recognize possible biases or limitations in AI-generated plans and ideas. By harnessing human expertise in interpreting AI insights, businesses can guarantee that AI-generated plans and ideas are based on practical experience and knowledge.

To effectively integrate AI into business planning and ideation, businesses must provide adequate training and support.

This includes training employees on how to use AI tools effectively, how to interpret AI insights, and how to integrate human input into AI-generated plans and ideas. By providing adequate training and support, businesses can ensure that employees are equipped with the knowledge and skills to effectively balance AI and human contributions.

Finding the right balance between AI and human contributions to business planning and ideation is critical for achieving optimal results. While AI offers tremendous opportunities for generating valuable insights and streamlining decision-making processes, it cannot replace the importance of human expertise and experience. Businesses must recognize the limitations and biases inherent in AI technology and implement strategies to ensure that human input is adequately integrated into the planning and ideation process. By doing so, businesses can leverage the strengths of both AI and human contributions to achieve better outcomes and remain competitive in an increasingly data-driven world.

Chapter 8 - Beyond Planning: Using AI for Implementation & Execution

Chapter 8

Using AI to Support Business Implementation & Execution

The role of artificial intelligence (AI) in business planning and decision-making is becoming increasingly prevalent. However, AI can also play a vital role beyond the planning phase, supporting the execution of business strategies and initiatives. In this chapter, we will discuss how businesses can leverage AI to support implementation and execution, including how it can help identify operational inefficiencies, automate repetitive tasks, and optimize resource allocation.

1. Identifying Operational Inefficiencies: AI can be a powerful tool for identifying operational inefficiencies and areas of improvement in business processes. For example, AI algorithms can analyze large data sets to identify patterns and trends that may indicate inefficiencies or bottlenecks. By identifying these areas of concern, businesses can take corrective action to improve operational efficiency and reduce costs.

2. Automating Repetitive Tasks: Another way AI can support business execution is by automating repetitive tasks. This can include anything from data entry to customer service interactions. By automating these tasks, businesses can free up employees to focus on more complex and strategic initiatives, while also increasing efficiency and reducing errors.

3. Optimizing Resource Allocation: AI can also be used to optimize resource allocation, helping businesses make better decisions about how to allocate their time, money,

and other resources. For example, AI algorithms can analyze customer data to identify the most profitable customer segments or the most effective marketing channels. This information can then be used to optimize resource allocation, ensuring that resources are allocated to the initiatives that are most likely to generate the greatest return on investment.

4. Improving Customer Experience: AI can also play a significant role in improving the customer experience, supporting business execution by providing personalized and targeted customer interactions. For example, AI-powered chatbots can provide customers with quick and accurate responses to common questions, reducing response times and improving customer satisfaction. Additionally, AI algorithms can analyze customer data to identify patterns and preferences, allowing businesses to provide more personalized and targeted marketing messages and product recommendations.

5. Predictive Maintenance: AI can also support business execution by enabling predictive maintenance of equipment and machinery. By analyzing data from sensors and other sources, AI algorithms can identify patterns that may indicate potential equipment failures. This can allow businesses to take corrective action before a failure occurs, reducing downtime and minimizing the costs associated with equipment repair or replacement.

6. Supply Chain Optimization: AI can also play a significant role in optimizing supply chain management, supporting business execution by providing real-time insights into inventory levels, shipment tracking, and delivery times. By leveraging this information, businesses can make more

informed decisions about inventory management, reducing waste and optimizing product availability.

7. Fraud Detection: AI can also be used to detect and prevent fraud, supporting business execution by identifying suspicious activity and transactions. For example, AI algorithms can analyze customer data to identify unusual patterns of behavior, such as unusually large purchases or purchases made from unusual locations. By detecting potential fraud early, businesses can take corrective action before significant losses occur.

8. Human Resource Management: AI can also play a role in human resource management, supporting business execution by providing insights into employee performance, engagement, and retention. For example, AI algorithms can analyze employee data to identify patterns and trends that may indicate low engagement or performance issues. This information can then be used to develop targeted training and development programs or to identify employees who may be at risk of leaving the organization.

Open-source resources can help businesses to effectively implement and execute AI solutions to support their operations. However, it is important to consider ethical considerations when using AI in business, and to ensure that these technologies are used in a responsible and transparent manner. Here are some of the more popular & effective options:

1. TensorFlow: TensorFlow is an open-source machine learning library developed by Google. It allows developers to build and train machine learning models, including those used for business applications.

2. Keras: Keras is another open-source machine learning library that simplifies the process of building and training deep learning models. It has a user-friendly interface and can be used with TensorFlow.

3. Scikit-learn: Scikit-learn is a popular machine learning library for Python that includes tools for data preprocessing, feature selection, and model selection. It can be used for a variety of business applications, including fraud detection and predictive maintenance.

4. Apache Mahout: Apache Mahout is a machine learning library that is designed to be scalable and efficient. It can be used for clustering, classification, and collaborative filtering.

5. H2O.ai: H2O.ai is an open-source platform for building and deploying machine learning models. It includes tools for data preparation, feature engineering, and model training.

6. Theano: Theano is a Python library that allows developers to define, optimize, and evaluate mathematical expressions. It is used primarily for deep learning applications.

7. Caffe: Caffe is an open-source deep learning framework that is designed for speed and efficiency. It can be used for a variety of business applications, including image and speech recognition.

8. Torch: Torch is an open-source machine learning library that is used primarily for deep learning applications. It includes several pre-built modules for building neural networks.

9. Apache Spark MLlib: Apache Spark MLlib is a machine learning library for Apache Spark, a distributed computing

system. It includes tools for data preprocessing, feature extraction, and model training.

10. PyTorch: PyTorch is a machine learning library that is primarily used for deep learning applications. It includes tools for building neural networks, as well as tools for visualization and data loading.

AI can play a critical role in supporting business execution, helping businesses identify operational inefficiencies, automate repetitive tasks, optimize resource allocation, improve the customer experience, enable predictive maintenance, optimize supply chain management, detect, and prevent fraud, and support human resource management.

By leveraging AI technology beyond the planning phase, businesses can gain valuable insights and efficiencies that can drive growth and profitability. However, it is important to recognize that AI is not a panacea and that human expertise and experience remain critical to successful business execution.

Chapter 8

Real World Examples of AI's Effect on Efficiency, Customer Engagement, and Business Operations

Artificial intelligence (AI) has been transformative in the world of business, providing organizations with new tools and approaches to improve operational efficiency, customer engagement, and other areas of business operations. In this chapter, we will explore several examples of how AI has been used to achieve these goals.

One area where AI has had a significant impact is supply chain management. AI can analyze large amounts of data from various sources, including social media, weather patterns, and transportation data, to predict demand and optimize inventory management. For example, Walmart has used AI to optimize its supply chain, reducing inventory carrying costs by 10% and increasing sales by 2%.

Another area where AI has been transformative is customer engagement. AI-powered chatbots can handle routine customer inquiries, freeing up human customer service representatives to focus on more complex issues. Additionally, AI can analyze customer data to personalize marketing campaigns and offer customized recommendations. For example, Sephora uses AI to provide customers with personalized product recommendations based on their skin tone, skin type, and other preferences.

AI has also been used to improve operational efficiency in manufacturing. By analyzing production data, AI can identify bottlenecks in the production process and suggest ways to improve efficiency. For example, Siemens uses AI to optimize the production of gas turbines, reducing production time by 20% and increasing capacity by 10%.

In the financial sector, AI has been used to detect and prevent fraud. By analyzing transaction data, AI can identify patterns and anomalies that may indicate fraudulent activity. For example, JP Morgan uses AI to detect fraudulent transactions, reducing false positives by 75%.

AI has also been used to improve healthcare outcomes. AI-powered systems can analyze medical data to identify patterns and predict health outcomes, enabling earlier diagnosis and treatment. For example, IBM Watson Health uses AI to analyze medical images and identify potential signs of breast cancer, improving the accuracy of diagnoses.

AI has even been used to optimize agriculture. By analyzing data on soil conditions, weather patterns, and other factors, AI can provide farmers with recommendations for optimizing crop yields. For example, the startup Taranis uses AI to analyze satellite imagery to identify areas of crops that may be stressed or require additional care.

AI has been transformative in improving operational efficiency, customer engagement, and other areas of business operations. From supply chain management to healthcare, AI has enabled organizations to analyze vast amounts of data and make data-driven decisions to optimize their operations. As the technology continues to evolve, businesses will have even more opportunities to leverage the power of AI to drive growth and improve their operations.

Chapter 8

How Can Businesses Effectively Leverage AI for Implementation & Execution?

As AI becomes more advanced and widely adopted, businesses are increasingly turning to it not just for planning and ideation, but also for implementation and execution. AI can help businesses improve operational efficiency, optimize resource allocation, improve customer engagement, and even enable predictive maintenance.

However, effectively leveraging AI for implementation and execution requires careful consideration and planning. In this chapter, we will discuss several key considerations for businesses looking to use AI beyond the planning phase.

Before implementing AI, businesses must first identify which areas of their operations can benefit from it. This may involve conducting an analysis of current business processes and identifying opportunities for automation, optimization, or improvement. By identifying the right processes to target, businesses can ensure that they are using AI in the most effective way possible.

To effectively leverage AI for implementation and execution, businesses must have access to high-quality, relevant data. This may involve cleaning and organizing existing data, or collecting new data through sensors, surveys, or other means. Additionally, data must be available in a format that is compatible with the AI algorithms being used.

Selecting the right AI technology and vendor is critical for successful implementation and execution. Different AI technologies are designed for different purposes, and not all vendors are created equal. Businesses must carefully evaluate their needs and consider factors such as cost, scalability, and ease of integration when choosing an AI vendor.

Integrating AI into existing workflows can be challenging, particularly if employees are not accustomed to working with it. Businesses must carefully consider how AI will fit into their existing processes and workflows and provide training and support to ensure that employees can work effectively with it.

Many industries are subject to regulations and standards that must be followed when implementing AI. Businesses must ensure that their use of AI is compliant with these regulations and standards, which may involve working with legal and regulatory experts.

As with planning and ideation, monitoring and evaluating AI performance is critical for successful implementation and execution. Businesses must continuously monitor accuracy, speed, and bias to ensure that AI is providing accurate and useful insights. By monitoring and evaluating AI performance, businesses can identify areas for improvement and adjust as necessary.

While AI can provide valuable insights, it is important to recognize that human expertise and experience remain critical to successful implementation and execution. Businesses must ensure that AI is being used in a way that complements human expertise, rather than replacing it. This may involve incorporating human feedback into AI algorithms or providing opportunities for employees to provide input on AI-generated insights.

As with planning and ideation, ensuring ethical use of AI is critical for successful implementation and execution. Businesses must ensure that AI is being used in a way that is fair and transparent and does not violate privacy or data protection regulations. Additionally, businesses must ensure that their use of AI does not contribute to bias or discrimination.

AI technology is constantly evolving, and businesses must be prepared to adapt to changes in technology and market conditions. This may involve revising business processes or workflows to take advantage of new AI capabilities or re-evaluating the use of AI considering changing market conditions.

Implementing AI can be disruptive, particularly if employees are resistant to change. Businesses must carefully manage change and resistance to ensure that employees are on board with the use of AI and understand its benefits.

AI has the potential to transform various areas of business operations, including operational efficiency, customer engagement, and human resource management. By leveraging AI beyond the planning phase, businesses can gain valuable insights, automate repetitive tasks, optimize resource allocation, improve the customer experience, enable predictive maintenance, optimize supply chain management, and detect and prevent fraud. However, effective AI implementation and execution require careful consideration of factors such as data quality, infrastructure, human expertise, and regulatory compliance.

By taking a thoughtful and strategic approach to AI implementation and leveraging the strengths of both AI and human expertise, businesses can unlock the full potential of AI and achieve greater growth and profitability. As AI continues to advance and evolve, businesses that embrace this technology will be better equipped to compete and succeed in the rapidly changing business landscape.

Chapter 8

Ethical Considerations

As businesses increasingly turn to AI for planning and ideation, it is important to consider the ethical implications of this technology. While AI has the potential to drive significant business value, it also presents new ethical challenges that must be addressed to ensure that its use is responsible and socially beneficial.

One of the primary ethical considerations in the use of AI for business planning and ideation is the potential for bias. AI systems are only as unbiased as the data used to train them, and if this data contains biases, the AI system will replicate and potentially amplify these biases. To mitigate this risk, businesses must ensure that the data used to train AI systems is representative and diverse, and that the algorithms used to generate insights are transparent and explainable.

Another key ethical consideration in the use of AI for business planning and ideation is privacy. AI systems often require access to large amounts of data, and businesses must ensure that this data is collected and used in accordance with applicable privacy laws and regulations. Additionally, businesses must take steps to secure this data and prevent unauthorized access, both to protect the privacy of individuals and to prevent potential misuse of sensitive information.

Transparency is also an important ethical consideration in the use of AI for business planning and ideation. AI-generated insights can have significant impacts on business decisions, and it is important that these insights are transparent and explainable so that decision-makers can understand how they were generated and make informed decisions. This can also help to build trust with stakeholders and customers who may be skeptical of the use of AI.

Another important ethical consideration in the use of AI for business planning and ideation is accountability. Businesses must be accountable for the decisions made based on AI-generated insights and must ensure that these decisions align with ethical and social values. Additionally, businesses must be transparent about the use of AI in decision-making and be prepared to address concerns or criticisms from stakeholders and customers.

Finally, the use of AI for business planning and ideation raises important ethical questions about the role of humans in decision-making. As AI becomes increasingly sophisticated, it may be tempting to rely solely on AI-generated insights and recommendations. However, it is important to recognize that human expertise and judgment remain critical to successful decision-making, and that AI should be used as a tool to augment and support human decision-making rather than replace it.

The use of AI for business planning and ideation presents new ethical challenges that must be addressed to ensure that its use is responsible and socially beneficial. To mitigate risks related to bias, privacy, transparency, accountability, and the role of humans in decision-making, businesses must take a thoughtful and strategic approach to the use of AI and incorporate ethical considerations into their AI strategy. By doing so, businesses can unlock the full potential of AI while also contributing to a more ethical and socially responsible use of this technology.

Chapter 9: Conclusion

Conclusion

Key Takeaways

Artificial Intelligence (AI) has revolutionized various industries, including business planning and ideation. As the world becomes increasingly data-driven, companies need to leverage AI to gain a competitive edge. While traditional market research methods have their place, they may not always result in unique or innovative ideas. AI-powered market research can quickly sift through vast amounts of data to identify gaps in existing markets that traditional methods may miss. AI can help businesses identify emerging trends and areas of consumer demand, providing valuable insights that can lead to new and innovative business ideas. However, as with any emerging technology, there are limitations and potential issues to consider when using AI in business planning and ideation. This section provides from the previous chapters:

- AI can help entrepreneurs with the ideation and planning process by providing valuable insights and intelligence that traditional methods may miss.
- AI can be used for market analysis, demand forecasting, supply chain management, risk assessment, and other aspects of running a successful business.
- AI can assist in creating a solid business plan by automating financial analysis, conducting predictive analytics, conducting market analysis and competitor analysis, assessing potential risks, and improving decision-making.

- AI-generated business ideas and plans have potential issues such as lack of human creativity, potential for bias, lack of context, overreliance on technology, and potential data privacy issues.
- Human input and expertise are necessary in business operations to ensure the accuracy, unbiasedness, and representation of the data used to train AI systems.
- Tips for incorporating AI into business planning processes include identifying business goals and needs, evaluating available resources, choosing the right AI tools, integrating AI with existing processes, and planning for scalability.
- Common challenges and limitations of AI in business planning include understanding the limitations of AI, combining AI with human expertise, addressing potential biases, ensuring data quality and accuracy, managing, and protecting data privacy and security, and ensuring compliance with industry regulations and ethical standards.

As the use of AI in business planning and ideation continues to grow, entrepreneurs need to be aware of the benefits, limitations, and potential issues associated with AI. AI has the power to transform how companies approach market research, ideation, and business planning. It can help businesses stay ahead of the competition, identify new markets, and create innovative solutions to longstanding problems. However, AI is not a panacea, and its limitations and potential ethical concerns must be considered.

By balancing the use of AI with human input and expertise, entrepreneurs can maximize the benefits of AI and achieve long-term success in their business ventures. As AI technology continues to advance, its potential to shape the future of business planning and ideation is limitless.

Conclusion

Final Thoughts on the Potential AI Impact on the Future of Business

As we conclude this book, we have explored the potential impact of Artificial Intelligence (AI) on the future of business. We have seen how AI can bring significant benefits, such as finding niche opportunities, increased efficiency, improved decision-making, and reduced costs. At the same time, we have also discussed some of the challenges and concerns associated with AI, including the ethical implications and potential job displacement.

Looking forward, AI will certainly continue to play a significant role in the future of business. With the continued development and implementation of AI technology, businesses will need to adapt to stay competitive. AI will become more prevalent across a variety of industries, and those who fail to embrace it risk being left behind.

One of the critical factors that will determine the success of AI in business will be its ability to complement human capabilities rather than replace them entirely. It is essential to remember that AI is a tool, and its effectiveness will ultimately depend on how it is used. Companies that can effectively integrate AI into their workflows while maintaining a focus on human-centered decision-making are likely to see the most significant benefits.

Another important consideration is the ethical implications of AI. As AI becomes more prevalent, it will be essential for businesses to ensure that their use of AI aligns with ethical principles and values. This includes issues such as data privacy, algorithmic bias, and transparency in decision-making.

While there is still much to be learned about the potential impact of AI on the future of business, we are at a turning point. The decisions we make today regarding the use of AI will have significant implications for the future of work and society. As we move forward, it will be crucial to balance the benefits of AI with ethical considerations and human-centric decision-making.

In conclusion, AI has the potential to revolutionize the way we do business, bringing with it a host of benefits and opportunities. However, it is important to approach this technology with caution and a critical eye. As we continue to explore the possibilities of AI, we must remember to keep our focus on what truly matters: creating a better future for all.

Comprehensive List of Artificial Intelligence Tools & Resources

There are a plethora of tools and platforms available to data scientists and machine learning practitioners to build and deploy their models. From open-source machine learning frameworks like TensorFlow, PyTorch, and MXNet to cloud-based platforms like Amazon SageMaker and Microsoft Azure Machine Learning Studio, there is no shortage of options.

Additionally, there are several business intelligence and analytics platforms like Tableau, Looker, and QlikView that can be used for visualizing and analyzing data. In this list, we've compiled some of the most popular and useful tools and platforms for data science and machine learning, including their descriptions and use cases.

- TensorFlow - An open-source machine learning framework developed by Google that can be used for developing, training, and deploying machine learning models.
- PyTorch - An open-source machine learning framework developed by Facebook that is widely used for building neural networks.
- Keras - An open-source neural network library written in Python that runs on top of TensorFlow or Theano.
- H2O.ai - An open-source machine learning platform that can be used for building and deploying machine learning models.

- IBM Watson Studio - A cloud-based data science platform that provides tools for building, training, and deploying machine learning models.
- Microsoft Azure Machine Learning Studio - A cloud-based machine learning platform that provides tools for building, training, and deploying machine learning models.
- Amazon SageMaker - A cloud-based machine learning platform that provides tools for building, training, and deploying machine learning models.
- Google Cloud AI Platform - A cloud-based machine learning platform that provides tools for building, training, and deploying machine learning models.
- DataRobot - An automated machine learning platform that can be used for building, training, and deploying machine learning models.
- Big Panda - An AIOps platform that can be used for incident management, root cause analysis, and proactive detection of issues.
- Sisense - A business intelligence and analytics platform that can be used for visualizing and analyzing data.
- Looker - A business intelligence and analytics platform that can be used for exploring and analyzing data.
- Tableau - A business intelligence and analytics platform that can be used for visualizing and analyzing data.
- QlikView - A business intelligence and analytics platform that can be used for exploring and analyzing data.
- Databricks - A cloud-based platform for building and deploying machine learning models.

- Dataiku - A collaborative data science platform that can be used for building, training, and deploying machine learning models.
- RapidMiner - A platform for building, training, and deploying machine learning models.
- SAS - A suite of analytics and data science tools that can be used for building and deploying machine learning models.
- Alteryx - A platform for data preparation, blending, and advanced analytics.
- Snowflake - A cloud-based data warehousing platform that can be used for storing and analyzing large amounts of data.
- Apache Spark - An open-source data processing engine that can be used for building and deploying machine learning models.
- MLflow - An open-source platform for managing the end-to-end machine learning lifecycle.
- Databand - A platform for managing data pipelines and machine learning workflows.
- Kubeflow - An open-source platform for building and deploying machine learning models on Kubernetes.
- Cognitivescale - A platform for building and deploying AI-powered enterprise applications.
- DataRobot AI Catalog - A platform for managing and discovering machine learning models.
- AWS Glue - A managed extract, transform, and load (ETL) service that can be used for preparing and transforming data.

- Hadoop - An open-source distributed computing framework that can be used for storing and processing large amounts of data.
- Azure HDInsight - A cloud-based managed Hadoop service that can be used for storing and processing large amounts of data.
- Google Cloud Dataproc - A cloud-based managed Hadoop and Spark service that can be used for storing and processing large amounts of data.
- Apache Flink - An open-source stream processing engine that can be used for real-time data processing.
- Apache Kafka - An open-source distributed streaming platform that can be used for real-time data processing.
- Google Cloud Pub/Sub - A cloud-based messaging service that can be used for real-time data processing.
- Google Dialogflow - A conversational AI platform that enables businesses to build chatbots, virtual assistants, etc.

Here is a comprehensive list of recommended YouTube channels and tutorials that cover the use of artificial intelligence for identifying business opportunities. These channels and tutorials provide insightful and practical advice on how businesses can leverage the power of AI to identify potential opportunities and gain a competitive advantage. Whether you are a business owner, entrepreneur, or marketer, these resources will help you understand how AI can be used to analyze data, uncover patterns and trends, and make informed decisions that can drive growth and success.

- Two Minute Papers - AI and Business Opportunities: This YouTube channel provides short, easy-to-digest videos about AI research and applications, including AI for business opportunities.

- Sentdex - Machine Learning with Python for Business: This channel has a series of videos that cover machine learning with Python for business purposes. Topics include natural language processing, sentiment analysis, and more.
- AI Business - Artificial Intelligence in Business: This YouTube channel focuses exclusively on the intersection of AI and business. Videos cover topics like how AI is transforming different industries and how companies can use AI to their advantage.
- Siraj Raval - AI for Business Leaders: This channel has a series of videos that introduce AI for business leaders. The videos cover topics like data analysis, predictive analytics, and machine learning.
- IBM Watson - Artificial Intelligence in Business: IBM Watson's YouTube channel has a series of videos that focus on the use of AI in business. Topics include AI for customer service, AI in finance, and more.
- Google Cloud - AI for Business: Google Cloud's YouTube channel has a series of videos that cover AI for business, including how companies can use Google Cloud AI services to improve their operations.
- Udacity - Artificial Intelligence for Business Leaders: This channel provides a series of videos on AI for business leaders, including topics like data analysis, machine learning, and more.
- Stanford Graduate School of Business - AI and Machine Learning in Business: This YouTube channel has a series of videos that cover AI and machine learning in business,

including applications of AI in marketing, finance, and more.

- NVIDIA - AI in Business: This channel has a series of videos that cover AI in business, including case studies and examples of how companies are using NVIDIA's AI technology to improve their operations.
- Microsoft AI - AI for Business Leaders: This channel provides a series of videos on AI for business leaders, including topics like machine learning, data analytics, and more.

Lastly, here are some additional resources you may find helpful:

- Coursera: Coursera is an online learning platform that offers courses on a wide range of topics, including artificial intelligence and business. You can find courses taught by experts in the field that cover everything from the basics of AI to advanced machine learning techniques.
- Kaggle: Kaggle is a platform for data scientists and machine learning engineers to compete in challenges, collaborate on projects, and share knowledge. It's a great resource for learning about AI and getting hands-on experience with real-world datasets.
- AI Business: AI Business is a website that covers news and trends in the AI industry, with a focus on how AI is being used in business. They offer insights, analysis, and case studies that can help you stay up-to-date on the latest developments and best practices.
- Harvard Business Review: The Harvard Business Review is a leading publication for business leaders and

managers. They frequently publish articles on AI and its impact on business, including how to identify new opportunities and strategies for incorporating AI into your organization.

- Data Science Central: Data Science Central is a community for data science professionals, with resources on AI, machine learning, and other related topics. They offer articles, tutorials, and forums where you can connect with other professionals and learn from their experiences.

I hope you find these resources helpful! I wish you best of luck in finding your unique niche opportunity.

Hello There

A Message from The Author

Dear Reader,

Thank you for taking the time to *The GPT-Reneur: Using Artificial Intelligence to Unlock Profitable Niches*. I hope you found it informative and helpful in your own journey as an entrepreneur.

As an author, the feedback I receive from readers like you is invaluable in helping me to continue to improve my writing and create content that is relevant and useful. That's why I would like to ask you to take a few minutes to leave a rating and review on the Amazon.

Not only does your review help me to know what I'm doing right and where I can improve, but it also helps other readers who are considering purchasing the book to make an informed decision. Your words have the power to influence others and to help them succeed in their own journey.

I would greatly appreciate your honest feedback, whether it's positive or negative. Your insights will not only help me to become a better writer, but they will also help other readers to benefit from the knowledge and experience that I've shared in this book.

Thank you again for your support and for taking the time to leave a review. It means the world to me.

Best regards,

Alex

www.ingramcontent.com/pod-product-compliance
Lightning Source LLC
Chambersburg PA
CBHW070604220526
45467CB00003B/1295